Managing Editor
Karen J. Goldfluss, M.S. Ed.

Editor-in-Chief
Sharon Coan, M.S. Ed.

Illustrators
Howard Chaney
Bruce Hedges

Cover Artist
Lesley Palmer

Art Coordinator
Kevin Barnes

Art Director
CJae Froshay

Imaging
James Edward Grace
Rosa C. See

Product Manager
Phil Garcia

Publisher
Mary D. Smith, M.S. Ed.

P9-AQE-588

Plants

SUPER SCIENCE ACTIVITIES

Written by Ruth M. Young, M.S. Ed.

Teacher Created Resources, Inc.
6421 Industry Way
Westminster, CA 92683
www.teachercreated.com

ISBN: 978-0-7439-3665-1

©2002 Teacher Created Resources, Inc.
Reprinted, 2009
Made in the U.S.A.

Table of Contents

Introduction

Plants grow in almost every part of the world—mountaintops, oceans, deserts, and polar regions. Plants have amazing abilities to adapt to many different environments, much as insects have done. Without plants, there would be no life on Earth. They provide the air we breathe and the food humans and other animals eat. Plants also supply us with many useful products such as lumber and cotton fibers.

Scientists believe there are more than 350,000 species of plants. Their size varies from barely visible plants that grow on the forest floor to the largest living life forms on Earth, giant sequoia trees of California. Some are more than 290 feet (88 m) high and over 30 feet (9 m) wide. Plants are also the oldest living things on Earth. One bristlecone pine tree in California started growing 4,000 to 5,000 years ago.

Plants develop from a tiny form called an embryo, which is usually contained within a seed. Seeds vary in size; the tobacco seed is so small that more than 2,500 grow in a pod less than 3/4 inch (19 mm) long. The largest seed is the coconut, which may weigh up to 20 pounds (9 kg). The seed provides food for the embryo plant until it can push its leaves above ground and begin to manufacture its own food. This is done from air, sunlight, and water by a process known as photosynthesis. Roots bring nourishment to the plant by absorbing dissolved minerals from the soil and water. Seeds require warmth, moisture, and oxygen to grow. The stages of a sprouting seed, called *germination*, are shown below.

Seed Germination

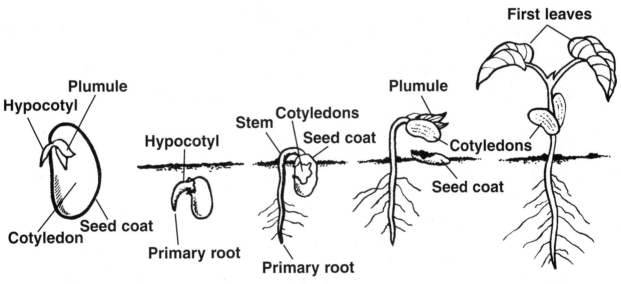

Cross section of a seed shows the embyro in a seed coat.

The seed splits and the hypocotyl forms the primary root.

As the root grows down, the stem breaks through the soil.

The cotyledons free the plumule, and the seed coat drops off.

As the stem grows upward, the plumule forms the first leaves.

The activities in this book are designed to provide students with opportunities to observe a wide variety of plants. This will begin with a search for seeds at school and home. Students gather data as they observe seeds germinating and do simple research on growing plants in different environments. Other methods of growing plants from parent plants (*cloning*) are explored using yams, carrots, begonia leaves, and pineapple. Seeds and flowers are dissected to discover their parts. Finally, students create models of flowers and plants and then learn the importance of bees to plants.

Is This a Seed?

Overview: *Students will sort a variety of materials to learn how to identify seeds.*

Materials

- variety of seeds (including seeds from fruits such as avocado, orange, and apple) These may be purchased in packets at a nursery. They will be used in the next activity as well.
- small objects which may look like seeds (e.g., Styrofoam pellets, marbles)
- paper plates
- blank file cards

Lesson Preparation

- Mix the materials to be used in sorting for seeds (listed above).
- Divide this among paper plates for groups of students to sort.
- copies of page 5 (one per group)

Activity

1. Give each student a blank file card and have each draw a seed on it. Do not give them any help since this is a pretest. Have them share their drawings and tell what they think a seed looks like. Collect the cards to use in a later lesson.

2. Explain that students are going to do an activity to see if they can tell seeds from things which are not seeds. Divide the students into small groups and distribute a plate of the mixture to each group. Give each group a copy of page 5. Discuss the sorting sheet with them so they see that there are three choices for the things they will sort. Tell them to take turns putting each item from the paper plate into the box in which they think it belongs.

3. As students sort the items, encourage them to discuss objects with the group members if they are unsure of where each belongs. Tell them to put any item in the "?" box if the group cannot agree on classifying it as a seed or nonseed.

4. When all sorting has been done, have the groups move to another group's area and, without moving any of the items, see if they agree. Discuss the results of the sorting to find which items were in the "?" box and which items were placed in different categories by the groups. (Do not give the answers; this same activity will be repeated at the end of the study.)

Closure

- Take students on a "seed hunt" around the school grounds. Collect seeds, if permitted, and then bring them into the classroom to begin a display of seeds. Include nonseed items which the students may have thought were seeds. Set aside a table area where students can display the seeds and nonseeds they collected.

- Send home the parent letter requesting that seeds be sent to school to help in this study. Add these to the seed display table. Put some strange seeds (e.g., a coconut) in the display.

Is This a Seed? *(cont.)*

Sorting Sheet

Instructions: Look at each object on the plate and put it in one of the boxes below. If you are not sure if it is seed or nonseed, put it in the "?" box.

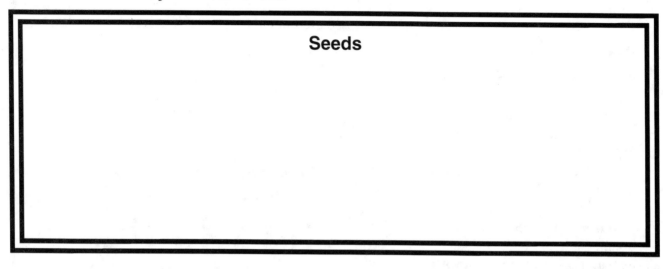

Seeds

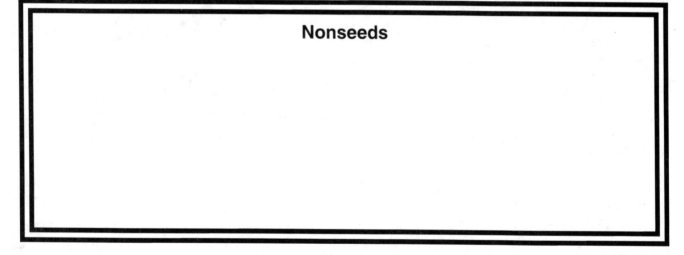

Nonseeds

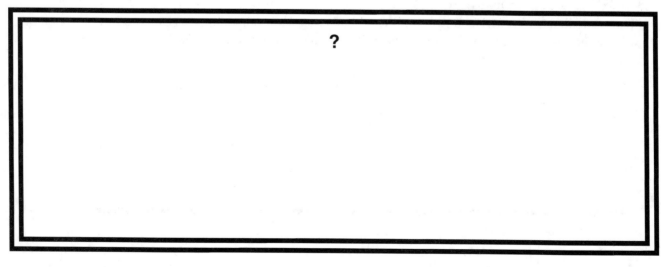

?

Parent Letter

Date_____

Dear Parents,

We have begun our study of plants by sorting a variety of materials to find seeds. Our class also went for a walk around the school grounds to search for seeds. The boys and girls are still learning the differences between seeds and nonseeds. Each of them has been asked to look around the house and outside in the yard to find examples of what they think might be seeds to bring to class. Please help them in this assignment but do not tell them whether an item is a true seed or not. They might look for seeds in some of the following places:

Where can I find seeds?

- cereal
- bushes
- soil
- spices used in cooking
- flowers
- trees

The students have been asked to bring these seeds to school during this week. We have a special area dedicated to our collection of seeds and nonseeds. These will be sorted later after we have learned more about seeds.

As always, you are welcome to come visit our classroom and see this display.

Thank you for your help with our study of seeds.

Cordially,

_____

Can You Match This?

Overview: *Students will match seeds with those from seed packets.*

Materials

- 30 different packets of seeds with pictures of the plants they will become (Select examples of large and small seeds. You should have more seeds than there are students.)
- white glue
- blank file cards
- cards with seed pictures drawn by students in Is This a Seed? activity (page 4).
- *optional:* whole coconut

Lesson Preparation

- Glue an example of the seed from each packet near the picture of the plant on the package.
- Number the file cards 1–30 and glue an example of each seed to them. Keep a record of the seed glued to each card.
- Spread seed packets around the room in reach of students.

Activity

1. Give each student a blank file card and have each draw a picture of a seed. Give them the pictures they drew in the first lesson (page 4) and have them compare their pictures. Collect the cards and save them for future use.
2. With the students, review the seed collection on the display table. Divide collections into two parts, one for seeds and the other for nonseeds. Have students take turns sorting items. If students cannot agree on where to place an item, put it in a separate area of the table and label the area with a question mark.
3. Ask students where seeds come from. (Many will have no idea or think they only come from stores.) Explain that they are about to play a matching game with seeds you have purchased.
4. Give each student a card with a seed glued to it. Show them where you have placed the seed packets. Tell them that they are going to move about the room, looking for the seeds which match the seed glued to their card. When they find it, they should take the seed packet and their card and return to their seats.
5. Let the students begin their search to match their seeds. If two students claim the same packet, have them examine their seeds carefully, perhaps using a magnifier, to see which seed it matches. This activity will improve the observation skills of the students since some of the seeds will look very much alike.
6. When all seeds have been matched, have students return their seed packets. Collect their seed cards in a basket or box. Mix up the cards and let students draw another seed card. If they get the same one as before, let them choose another from the box.

Closure

- Have the students sit in small groups and examine their seeds to find what they have in common. They will find that some seeds look alike, while others look very different.
- *Optional:* Show them the coconut and explain that it is the largest seed of all. Crack it open and let them taste a bite.

Making Pictures from Seeds

Overview: *Students will use a variety of seeds to create pictures.*

Materials

- seeds from the seed packets used in the lesson "Can You Match This?"
- white glue which will dry clear
- 4-inch (10 cm) square of cardstock (colored if possible), one per student
- small paper plates
- toothpicks (one per student)
- *optional:* pair of tweezers per group

Lesson Preparation

- Place the seeds on small paper plates to be distributed to student groups.

Activity

1. Divide the students into small groups and provide each of them with a set of seeds, glue, toothpicks, and cardstock pieces. Tell each student to make a large drawing of an animal or insect (e.g., butterfly), like those used in coloring books. Explain that they will be filling in this drawing with seeds which will be glued in place.

2. Let the students practice placing some seeds on their picture before gluing to see how close these need to be in the picture. After they are ready, tell them to spread a small amount of glue with the toothpick on one part of their picture and then add seeds. They may use the tweezers to move the seeds if needed.

3. Permit enough time for the students to do a good job, since this will take practice and patience. This lesson may be spread over several sessions in order to let the students have time to do their best work.

Closure

- Display the seed pictures on a bulletin board.
- Make picture frames to enhance the seed pictures. Cut a piece of construction paper one inch (2.5 cm) larger in diameter than the cardstock piece. Lay the cardstock in the center of the paper and then trace around it with a pencil. Remove the cardstock, turn it over and then fold along the creases so the edges of the paper stand up to form a box. Crease each corner at an angle to complete the frame. Glue the seed picture into the bottom of the box frame.

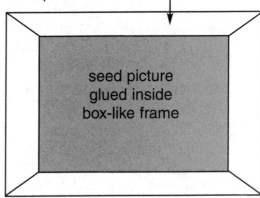

construction paper folded up around seed picture like a box

seed picture glued inside box-like frame

What's Inside a Seed?

Overview: *Students will dissect seeds to find the embryo plant inside.*

Materials

- large lima beans (two for each student)
- peanuts in the shell (enough for each student plus extras)
- magnifier for each student
- blank file cards
- bowl of water

Lesson Preparation

- Soak lima beans for at least three hours prior to this lesson. Keep enough dry beans for all to have one for comparison.

Activity

1. Distribute a file card and dry lima bean to each student. Have them fold the card in half. Tell them to draw the outline of the lima bean on one half the card. Draw a model on the board so they will know to make outlines large enough to fill half the card.

2. Tell the students to draw within the bean outline what they think is inside the lima bean.

3. Distribute a soaked bean and magnifier to each student. Show them how to peel off the outer skin and set it aside. Ask them what they think the skin does for the seed. (*It protects the seed just as their own skin does.*)

4. The seed will now begin to open. Caution students that what they are looking for inside the seed will be very tiny and the same color as the seed. Have them look carefully between the two halves of the seed to find the tiny embyro plant. (*It will consist of a thick root and two flattened leaves with veins.*)

5. Have students use their magnifiers to examine the small plant. Help them to find details. Tell them to make another outline of the lima bean seed on the other half of their file card and draw the tiny plant which they see inside their seed.

Closure

- Ask the students if they think that a tiny plant is inside every seed. (*Many may think that only the lima bean has these.*) Distribute a peanut in the shell to each student. Ask them if peanuts are seeds. (*Most will be unsure*). Explain that nuts are seeds. Have them open the peanut shell to look inside. Let them peel off the skin, reminding them that this is just like the lima bean skin. Have the students open the peanuts carefully to see if there is a tiny plant inside. If they look closely, they will see that in fact there is a small plant.

- Ask students again if they think that a small plant is inside each seed. Tell them that baby plants live off material inside a seed until they grow into a plant and can make food for themselves. Tell students to eat the peanuts so they can see that people can eat the food in these seeds and get nourishment from it just as the baby plant would.

- Give students their original seed drawings and have them make new drawings on the same card. Let them compare what they have learned about seeds since they made the first drawing.

Where Do Seeds Come From?

Overview: *Students will examine a variety of plants to find seeds. They will also eat some seeds.*

Materials

- assortment of nuts
- variety of fresh fruits and vegetables (e.g., banana, apple, orange, avocado, corn, tomato)
- knife
- paper plates and clear plastic wrap
- mixture of seeds, nonseeds, and sorting sheets from Is This a Seed? activity (pages 4 and 5)

Lesson Preparation

- Lay the nuts and fruits on a table where students may gather to see them. Have these on display as students enter the classroom and allow them to look at these before beginning.

Activity

1. Divide the students into small groups and have each of them think of three from things they have learned about seeds. Tell them to take turns sharing these in their groups. Discuss some of the major concepts about seeds which they described in groups.
2. Gather the students around the table with nuts and fruits displayed. Ask them from where they think seeds come. Tell them that everything on the table is a seed or has a seed inside it.
3. Show the nuts and let students eat them. Ask them to tell what is inside each nut (*embyro plant*).
4. Show them the fruits and vegetables and ask what is inside them. (*Not all students will realize that seeds are found in them.*) Cut each of these open, wrap them in plastic wrap, and put them on separate paper plates. Pass them around so all the students can examine them. Be sure they find the location of the seeds in each of the samples.
5. Have the students tell which seeds they have eaten along with the accompanying fruits and vegetables (e.g., banana or tomatoes) and which seeds are removed rather than eaten (e.g., orange or pumpkin). If you use an ear of corn as an example, point out that the only parts we eat are the kernels—seeds.
6. Cut small pieces of the fruits and vegetables which can be eaten raw and let the students taste these.

Closure

- Distribute the mixture of seed and nonseeds to the students along with the sorting sheet used in Is This a Seed? at the beginning of this study. Let them sort the materials again and compare this with the first time they did this activity.
- As homework, ask students to look for seeds they might eat with their evening meal or tomorrow's breakfast. Have them write to their parents saying that they are to tell the class what seeds they eat for dinner or breakfast. Include an invitation to the parents to help them identify these and perhaps send a sample of the seeds for their child to show the class.

How Do Seeds Grow?

Overview: *Students will plant various seeds to observe them grow.*

Materials

- pinto beans
- lima beans
- clear plastic cups (9–10 oz)
- roll of paper towels
- soldering iron or other tool which gets hot

- metric ruler
- permanent ink marker
- copies of the data sheet Seed Growth Record (page 12)

Lesson Preparation

- With a hot tool such as a soldering iron, melt several holes in the bottom of the clear plastic cups. These are drainage holes since the cups will be used for growing seeds.
- Soak the lima beans and pinto beans for an hour prior to beginning. Each student will need one of each of these beans.

Activity

1. Distribute the file cards with the seeds drawn on them. Review with the students what they saw inside the seeds. Ask them what they think happens to a seed when it is planted. (Do not describe a growing seed; they will discover this on their own.)

2. Divide the class into groups of two or three students. Distribute a lima and a pinto bean (seed) to each student. Give each group a plastic cup and three paper towels. Have the students fold one paper towel in thirds lengthwise and line the wall of the cup with it. They should form a ball with the other two towels and push them into the center of the cup to support the first towel. Add enough water to dampen the paper towels, letting excess drain off.

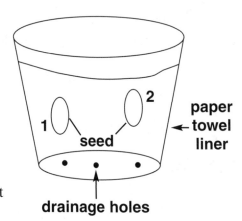

3. Have each child push the two seeds about halfway down the cup between the paper and the wall but still visible through the cup. Number the seeds in each cup, using the permanent felt pen.

4. Distribute the Seed Growth Record to each student and have each complete the information. Have them place today's date under the first cup and then draw their seeds.

5. Students should make drawings every day to show the growth of their seeds. Give each a folder in which to keep this record, as well as other data they will be keeping during the study of plants. These will be placed in a plant journal at the end of the study.

Closure

- This project will take several weeks. During that time, students should continue their records of the growth of the plants. Discuss what happens as the plants grow, such as the development of the two leaves which were inside the seeds and the withering of the original seed once it is no longer needed.

How Do Seeds Grow? *(cont.)*

Seed Growth Record

Name: _____ Lima Bean Seed #_____ Pinto Bean Seed #_____

To the Student: Make a drawing each day to show what happens to your seeds as they grow. When the stems begin to grow, measure them and write their length under the containers.

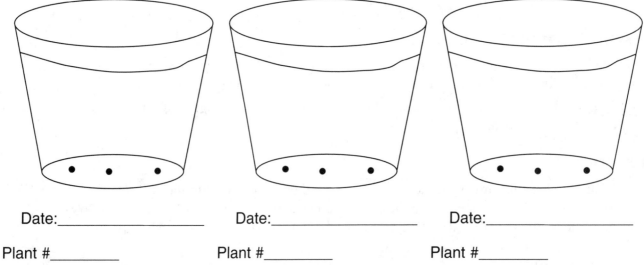

Date:_____   Date:_____   Date:_____

Plant #_____   Plant #_____   Plant #_____

Length of stem:_____cm   Length of stem:_____cm   Length of stem:_____cm

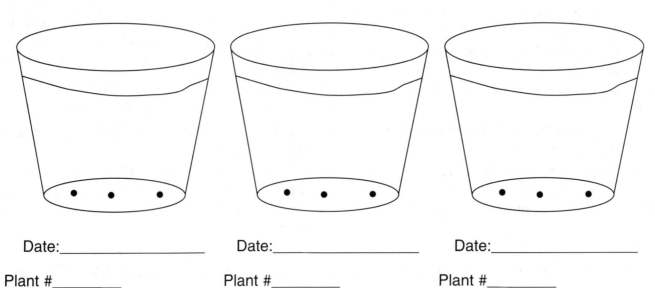

Date:_____   Date:_____   Date:_____

Plant #_____   Plant #_____   Plant #_____

Length of stem:_____cm   Length of stem:_____cm   Length of stem:_____cm

How Do Plants Grow?

Overview: *Students will graph the growth of bean seeds and plant other seeds.*

Materials

- bean seeds planted in previous lesson
- Seed Growth Graph (page 14)
- magnifier for each student

Lesson Preparation

- Keep students in the same groups throughout this study of plants so they continue to work together to record plant growth. This activity should be done when the stems on most of the plants are at least 3/4" (2 cm) long.
- If any seeds begin to rot, remove them so they will not contaminate the remaining seeds.

Activity

1. Have students compare the growth of their plants. Be sure they notice that although all seeds were planted at the same time, not all plants have grown to the same height.
2. Let students compare the growth of leaves on their plants to see what is alike and what is different for the two plants. Have them compare leaves on all plants being raised by the groups.
3. Distribute a copy of page 14 to all students. Show them how and where to place today's date on the graph. Let them add the rest of the dates, including nonschool days, to their graph.
4. Demonstrate how they should plot the length of the stem for each of their plants on the same date line. Let them use a different colored pen to represent each of the plants. They should make a line beside the pinto and lima bean words to show the color being used for each of them. This same color should then be used to go over the dots on the graph that represent each plant.
5. The growth of each plant should be measured daily and plotted on the graph. When there are nonschool days, data is extrapolated by plotting the plant's growth on the next school day following the nonschool days. The points for the two data are then connected. Students will realize that growth took place, even though they were not there to measure it. They can use the graph to read the growth which took place during the nonschool days.

Closure

- Have students make drawings of their plants on their Seed Growth Record chart. Make additional copies as needed.
- Have students measure and plot each plant's growth daily. Compare these with plants grown by other groups. This comparison lets them realize that plants do not all grow in the same way.

How Do Plants Grow? *(cont.)*

Seed Growth Graph

To the Student: Your teacher will help you make a graph of the lima bean and pinto bean plants you are growing. Compare how these plants grow.

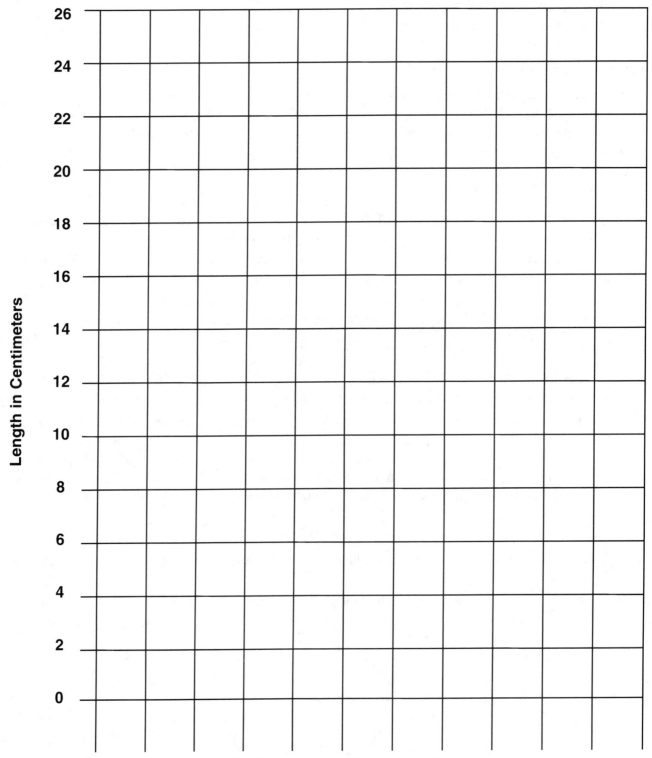

How Does Your Garden Grow?

Overview: *Students will plant a small garden of birdseed on a sponge.*

Materials

- untreated birdseed
- untreated sponges (one per group)
- aluminum pie pan (one per group)
- Birdseed Growth Data Sheet (page 16)

- magnifier for each student
- water
- hot-glue gun

Lesson Preparation

- Label the pie pans with a number which is assigned to each group of students. Hot-glue one sponge to each pie pan to keep it in place. Add enough water to soak the sponge and leave a thin covering of water on the bottom of the pan.

Activity

1. Have students get into their groups. Distribute a magnifier to each student and a sample of birdseed. Let them examine the birdseed and describe what they see. Tell them that these seeds are too small to open up to see if each has a baby plant inside it. Ask them to think of a way to find out if there is a baby plant inside. Tell them that one way is to plant them in a small garden where they can be observed.

2. Provide each group with a pie pan, sponge, and about a tablespoon of birdseed. Let the students sprinkle their birdseed over the top of the sponge. Tell them they have just planted a small garden. Explain that these will be collected and placed on a table but will be returned to each group daily during the time they measure their lima bean and pinto bean plants. Explain that they will keep a daily record of changes they see in their gardens.

3. Distribute a copy of page 16 to each student to begin the recording of the sponge garden.

Closure

- Record the growth of the seeds.

- Discuss what the students have learned thus far.

Extender

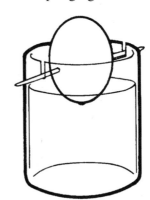

- Soak an avocado seed to soften it and split it open so the students can see the small seedling inside.

- Grow an avocado seed for students to observe. It takes several months for the seedling to appear. Use a one-pint (.5 L) water bottle cut to half its height. Push two toothpicks or T-pins into opposite sides of the seed about halfway between the ends. Cut two slits on opposite sides of the bottle and put the toothpicks in the slits. The seed should be suspended so the stem end is below water level. Replace the water as it evaporates.

How Does Your Garden Grow? *(cont.)*

Birdseed Growth Data Sheet

Name:_____ Date: _____

To the Student: You have just planted a small garden of birdseed on a sponge. Since you are doing an experiment to see if there is anything inside the seeds, it is important to make a record of what happens during the next few days. Begin your record on the chart below.

Birdseed Growth Record		
Date	**Tell what the seeds look like today.**	**Draw some of the seeds.**

Let's Experiment with Plants

Overview: *This activity is done when the bean plants are at least three inches (8 cm) high and the birdseed has developed sprouts. Students will conduct experiments with their plants to see how they grow under various conditions.*

Materials

- bean plants
- sponge gardens
- dark closet
- stack of books (or ring stand)
- two large shoeboxes
- pieces of tagboard
- clear tape

- liquid plant fertilizer
- bottle for water with liquid fertilizer
- plant record sheets begun in previous activities
- access to a refrigerator
- rulers or sticks
- *optional:* video camera

Lesson Preparation

- Use books (or a ring stand) and rulers (or sticks) to support one of the cups upside down with bean plants in it. Put clear tape across the cup opening to avoid having the paper towels drop out. The sponge garden will be supported in the same way. Since the sponge is glued to the pie pan, it will not fall out when it is inverted over the books. Place an empty pie pan below each of these to catch the run-off water. Turn the planters over only to water them.

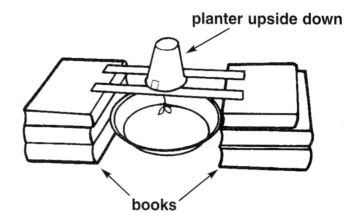

planter upside down

books

- The plants will begin to grow upward within 24 hours and should grow straight up within three days. Gravity causes this effect on plants, which is called *geotropism*. This experiment demonstrates what happens to trees growing on hillsides.

- Use one shoebox to create a container for one cup of bean plants. Put a hole in one end of the box, and two tagboard shelves on opposite sides of the walls of the box. The first should be just above the level of the top leaves, the second about halfway between this distance and the top of the box. Put the lid on the box. Open the box only to water the plants and for students to make drawings of the plant's growth.

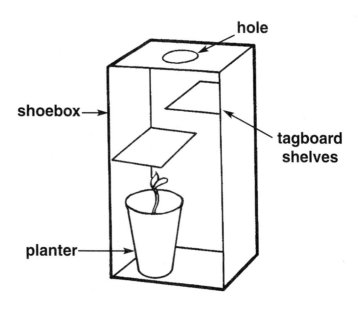

hole

shoebox

tagboard shelves

planter

Lesson Preparation *(cont.)*

- Use the other shoebox to make a container for the sponge garden. The box should lie flat. These plants will not grow to the height of the beans, but this darkness test will show which direction plants grow in order to reach light. Use a nail and poke four or five holes in one end of the box. Put the garden in the box and put the lid on the box. Have students open the books only to water the gardens and to make drawings of the plants' growth.

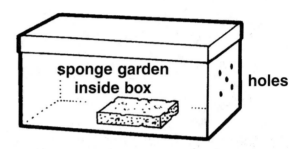

Activity

1. Divide students into their groups with their bean plants and birdseed gardens. Let them complete their records for these.

2. Ask students what plants need in order to be healthy. List these needs on the board, including light and water. Include other suggestions, even if not correct. Students will learn as they conduct their experiments what is needed by the plants.

3. Tell students that they are going to conduct some experiments to see what happens when plants are grown under different conditions. Explain that one of the cups of bean plants and a sponge garden will have no changes made (*control*)—that is, they will get the same amount of water and sunlight as they have thus far. Students will compare these with plants which are used in the experiments.

4. Write the list of changes (*variables*) to be used in the plant experiments on the board.

   - no sunlight
   - hanging upside down
   - inside a shoebox
   - inside a refrigerator
   - lying on one side
   - no water
   - fertilizer added
   - no change (*control*)

5. Discuss the various experiments which will be done. Explain that throughout the experiments, students will be keeping records of their plants' growth. They will also be watching the other plants to see what changes are occurring. Explain to students that the same experiments will be done with both the bean and birdseed plants to compare what happens.

6. Assign each group to do two different experiments. Use a different variable for each group's plants (e.g., no light and inside shoebox). On their bean and birdseed record sheets, have the students write the variable they will use with each plant.

7. Place the plants in the locations where they will be kept during the experiment (dark closet, shoebox, etc.) Mix fertilizer with water according to the directions on the container and pour it into a bottle. Label the bottle "Water with Fertilizer." Make this bottle available for the groups conducting that experiment.

Let's Experiment with Plants *(cont.)*

Closure

- *Optional:* Make a time-lapse videotape of some of the changes taking place. The bean plants hanging upside down will be the best ones to use for this recording. The gradual change of the bean stems will be dramatic as the videotape is played back.

- Conduct these experiments for at least two weeks. Chart plant growth and changes daily. Periodically, have each group share what they see happening with their plants.

Bean and Birdseed Plant Experiments	
Variable	**Expected Results**
no sunlight	• Stems will grow very long. • Leaves and stems will be pale.
lying on one side	• Stems will begin to grow upright. This is caused by gravity and is called *geotropism*.
hanging upside down	• Plants will gradually turn and then grow straight up. Compare this with the plants lying on their sides.
no water	• Plants will wither and leaves may change color.
inside shoebox	• Plants will grow toward the light.
fertilizer added	• Plants will grow rapidly and should look healthier than control plant.
inside refrigerator	• Plants will grow slowly and become pale. Compare these with the plants grown in the dark.

Leaf Rubbings

Overview: *Students will learn about the shapes and functions of leaves.*

Materials

- variety of leaves
- white paper (lightweight)
- crayons

Lesson Preparation

- Gather as many types of leaves as possible, with the students' assistance if possible. Divide the leaves into sets that contain a sample of each leaf type.
- Do a leaf rubbing to learn the technique and find the best method for presenting this activity to the students. (See Activity #4 for instructions.)

Activity

1. Divide the students into small groups and distribute a set of leaves to each of them. Tell the students to examine the leaves and then sort them into piles according to one characteristic (color, size, shape)

2. When the groups are finished sorting, have them rotate to another table and examine the piles of leaves to find out how they were sorted. Have one person from each group state what characteristic was used to sort the leaves. List the characteristics on the board.

3. Have the students sort the leaves left by the previous group, using another characteristic. In this way, they will become familiar with the various attributes of the leaves.

4. Distribute a piece of white paper to each student and provide them with crayons. Show them how to place one leaf beneath the paper, hold down firmly so it will not slip, and rub lightly with the side of the crayon over the surface of the leaf. They need to cover the entire leaf to see the outline of the veins and edges appear.

Closure

- Have students collect more leaves from home and do more rubbings with these as well. Put the rubbings on the bulletin board to display their work and to use in the next two lessons.
- Pin the leaves used in the rubbing activity, as well as others, to the bulletin board and have students find which ones match the rubbings.

Extender

- Have the students make rubbings of tree bark and add this to the display.

Cloning Plants

Overview: *Students will discover that new plants can sometimes grow from a parent plant without the need of a seed.*

Materials

- ripe whole pineapple
- whole yam (or sweet potato)
- carrot
- apple
- toothpicks
- two jars with openings, one to fit the yam, the other for the carrot
- pebbles
- healthy begonia leaf
- sand and potting soil
- untreated sponge
- aluminum pie pan
- flower pot with drainage hole
- knife
- water
- white plastic trash bag
- clear plastic bag
- house plant fertilizer

Activity

Have students observe the growth of new plants from parent plants. The plants to be used are a yam, carrot, begonia, and pineapple. This activity may extend over the entire school year. Prepare the plants as students watch. Place the plants where students can observe. Discuss the plants' growth periodically with students.

1. **Yam:** Place the yam in a container of water which has a mouth slightly larger than the yam's diameter and enough room for roots to form. Push four toothpicks into the yam about halfway between the tips. Half of the yam should be covered with water when placed in the jar. Change the water periodically. The roots will appear first, followed by the roots which emerge from the other end of the yam.

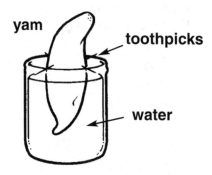

2. **Carrot:** Cut off all but two inches (5 cm) of the carrot. Trim off the sprouts on top of the carrot, leaving the green base. Follow the same directions used for the yam and suspend the carrot in a jar of water. The water should cover the bottom ¹/₂ inch (1 cm) of the carrot. Add water as needed. Within a week feathery, green sprouts should appear from the top of the carrot.

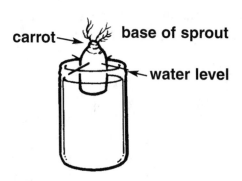

3. **Begonia:** Place the sponge in the pie pan and add enough water to soak the sponge and just cover the bottom of the pan. Use a large, healthy begonia leaf and make five cuts in the leaf from the outer edge into the main vein. Lay the leaf on top of the sponge, underside down. Place a few pebbles on the leaf to keep it near the damp sponge. Add water to the pan periodically to keep the sponge wet. New plants should emerge from the cuts within several weeks.

Activity *(cont.)*

4. **Pineapple:** Cut the top off a ripe pineapple to get a tuft of leaves and a bit of stalk. Carefully peel some of the lower leaves from the base of leaves to reveal more stem and some small bumps, perhaps even some baby roots which have started to grow beneath the leaves. Place the stem portion of this into a flower pot filled with potting soil which is about one-half sand. The potting soil will hold the water, and the sand will allow it to drain readily and allow sufficient oxygen into the soil.

Place the pot and plant in a white plastic garbage bag which is loosely sealed at the top. Put the plant where it will get six hours of sunlight, if possible. The bag keeps the humidity high and diffuses the light so the plant doesn't burn in the sunlight. If less sunlight is available, use a clear plastic bag. Water sparingly as the soil dries. Don't overwater, but don't let it go completely dry. Fertilize once or twice a month with a house plant fertilizer. New growth should appear at the top of the plant after about two months. If the base looks like it is rotting, start again with a new pineapple top and fresh potting soil and add less water.

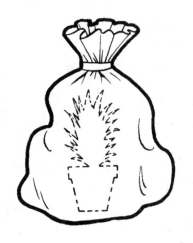

When the plant gets large, place an apple in the bag. The ripening apple produces ethylene gas which will induce flowering in the pineapple. You will have to continue these treatments for a couple of months, replacing the apple several times. It may take up to a year to get a new tiny pineapple.

Closure

- Have students make drawings to place in their plant journals to show how these plants looked when first planted.

- After the plants have begun to sprout new growth, have the students make other drawings to record the changes they observe.

Flower Power

Overview: *Students will dissect flowers to discover where seeds originate.*

Materials

- complete flower (e.g., lily, gladiola, or tulip)
- Flower Dissection Instructions and Parts-of-a-Flower Data Sheet (pages 24 and 25)
- clear tape
- magnifier
- transparency of How Flowers Reproduce (page 26)
- several apples

Activity

1. Ask the students if they know how seeds are produced. Tell them they are about to take a flower apart so they can see where seeds are formed. If the students are too young to dissect flowers alone, do this activity as a demonstration.

2. Distribute data sheets, flowers, magnifiers, and clear tape to students and let them follow the data sheets as they dissect the flower.

Closure

- Use the transparency How Flowers Reproduce (page 26) to explain the reproduction process to students. Tell them bees are the best pollinators of flowers. When a bee goes to a flower to get nectar and pollen, some pollen drops off the bee's body onto the sticky stigma on the pistil. Beekeepers often rent hives to farms with apple orchards or other trees needing to be pollinated. Other insects which visit flowers also pollinate them. Pollen can also be transferred to the stigma by wind and by some birds and bats.

- Explain that fruits and vegetables are really swollen ovaries of a blossom that grew on the plant. Show students an apple and point out the leftover blossom and stem on opposite ends. Cut the apple open to expose the seeds formed inside the ovary. Let the students examine the seeds.

- Save the students' flower parts to be used in the next lesson and in the plant journal.

Extender

- Take students on a walk to search for fruit-bearing plants that show blossoms and fruit. Try to find examples of the transition from blossom to fruit on a plant. Cut open a blossom to expose the swollen ovary inside, the beginning of the fruit.

- Have students examine a dandelion flower and one which has gone to seed. This is a great example of a composite flower. Each seed is formed in its own flower but combined with others.

Flower Power *(cont.)*

Flower Dissection Instructions

To the Student: Follow directions as you carefully dissect the flower.

- Snip off a piece of the stem. Examine it with the magnifier and then tape it in the box marked "stem" on the Parts-of-a-Flower Data Sheet. Complete the rest of the information in the box.

- Locate the *sepals*, *petals*, *stamens*, and *pistil*. Count their number and write this in the boxes.

- Gently pull off the sepals and tape a specimen in the sepal box. Describe how it feels.

- Smell the flower; if it has a fragrance, describe it in the petal box. Carefully remove the petals and tape one to the data sheet. Answer the question about the flower's color and fragrance.

- Examine a stamen, the male part of the flower. Look at the top of the stamen (*anther*) with a magnifier to see the pollen grains. Put your fingertip against the anther. Did the pollen stick to your finger? This is what happens when a bee touches it. Rub the pollen between your fingers and then describe what it feels like in the pollen box.

- Take a sample of pollen grains using the sticky side of a piece of clear tape. If you have a microscope, place the tape on a glass slide and examine it. Put a sample of pollen grains in the pollen box. Draw what the pollen grains look like when magnified.

- Remove the stamens and tape one of them in the box. Describe what you see on the anther and draw a magnified view of it.

- Study the pistil, the female part of the flower. Feel the stigma, the top of the pistil. Describe how it feels. At the bottom of the pistil is a swollen area (*ovary*). Try to cut it open with your fingernail. Use your magnifier to see if you can find any tiny seeds inside the ovary. You may be able to split the stem of the stigma (*style*) lengthwise to see if you can locate the pollen tube which has grown from the stigma to the ovary.

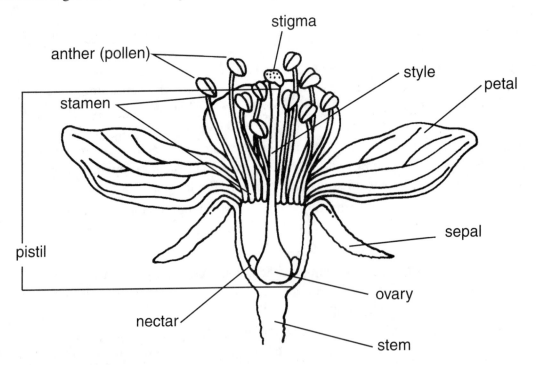

Flower Power *(cont.)*

Parts-of-a-Flower Data Sheet

To the Student: Tape the parts of the flower in the correct boxes below and then complete the information.

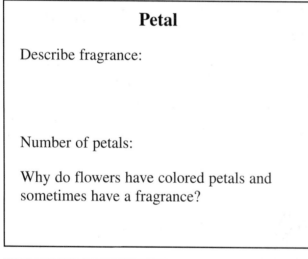

Stem

Description:

Magnified View
of the Tip of the Stem

Sepal

Number of sepals:

Description of how it feels:

Petal

Describe fragrance:

Number of petals:

Why do flowers have colored petals and sometimes have a fragrance?

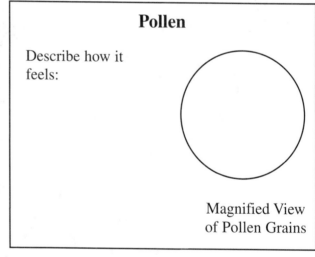

Pollen

Describe how it feels:

Magnified View
of Pollen Grains

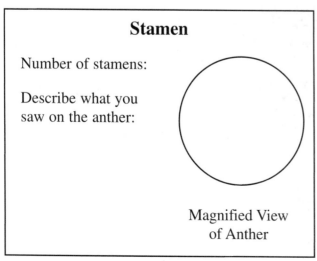

Stamen

Number of stamens:

Describe what you saw on the anther:

Magnified View
of Anther

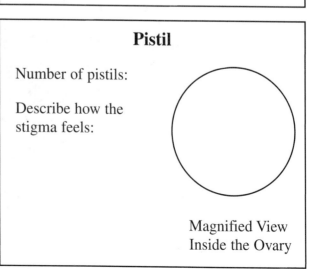

Pistil

Number of pistils:

Describe how the stigma feels:

Magnified View
Inside the Ovary

Flower Power *(cont.)*

How Flowers Reproduce

1. Each pollen grain is a single cell. Pollen forms on the top (anther) of the stamen.
2. Pollen is carried by insects, wind, or birds to the stigma, the sticky top of the pistil.
3. Once on the stigma, the pollen grain absorbs moisture from the pistil and breaks open.
4. Its contents form a pollen tube, growing down into the pistil.
5. The pollen tube grows until it reaches the ovule containing an egg cell.
6. Sperm from the pollen travels down the tube to the ovule and unites with the egg cell.
7. A seed now begins to develop inside the ovary.
8. An ovary may have a single seed (avocado) or more than one seed (apple).
9. The ovary develops into a fruit enclosing the seed(s).

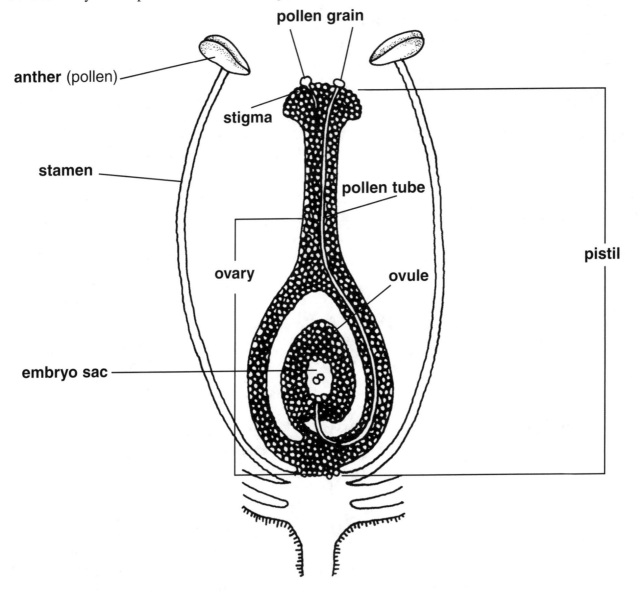

Coloring Plants

Overview: *Students will trace the flow of liquid through flowers and celery.*

Materials

- 2 white carnations
- 3 small containers
  (Drinking glasses or small vases work well.)
- 3 celery stalks with leaves
- string

- leaf rubbings from previous lesson
- dark blue and red ink
- red and blue crayons

Lesson Preparation

- Try the experiment with the flowers and celery before doing this with the students. This will help you know how long it will take to see the color change take place.
- Pour each ink into a separate container. Only a small amount is needed, enough to cover about 1 inch (2.5 cm) of the bottom of the stem.

Demonstration

1. Explain to the students that you are going to do a demonstration to show how a nutrient (food) travels through the plant and into the leaves of plants.

2. Cut the tips off the stems of the carnations and place the stems into one of the containers. Next, cut a small piece off the tips of each of the celery stalks. Split the stalks lengthwise to about half way to the leaves.

3. Place the celery stalks into the containers by lowering one half of the split stalk into the red-ink container and the other into the blue-ink container.

4. Let the flowers and celery sit in their containers as the students make observations. Have them make drawings of the plants at the beginning, and then add changes. Let students use red and blue crayons to show the changes as they appear. Eventually, the color will extend into the leaves of the celery and pedals of the carnation.

Closure

- Discuss how and where the plants changed color. Point out the leaf rubbing display and how this showed the veins in the leaves. Cut the celery stalks into short cross sections so student can see the ends of the veins. Pass these to the students for them to examine closely. They will notice the dark color has concentrated in the veins.
- Explain that the ink represents liquid that has dissolved nutrients from the soil that is drawn in by the plant roots and then makes its way to every part of the plant.

Extender

- If the bean plants are still being grown, mix ink with a small amount of water and water the plants with it, using the normal amount of the water. Have the students observe the plants over several days to see the color being drawn in by the roots and traveling up the plant to the leaves and coloring them.

Taking in Water and Minerals

Overview: *Students will do experiments to see the process which carries liquid into a plant.*

Materials

- 3 clear plastic or glass tubes of different diameters
- tissue for each student
- red or blue coloring (ink or food coloring will work well)
- clear container of water
- transparency of How Plants Get Their Food (page 29)
- string
- several balloons
- books
- yard (meter) stick
- masking tape
- paper
- pencils

Lesson Preparation

- Inflate the balloons and use string to hang them from the ceiling. Do not tell the students what these are used for but have them observe what happens to them over several days. (They will notice that the air appears to leak out of the balloon, even though it is sealed.)

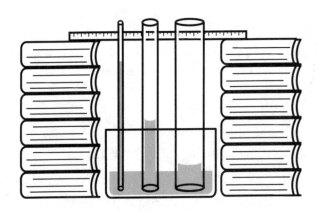

- Place books on either side of the container and rest a yardstick across the top of them. Tape the tubes to the stick without sealing their tops. The tubes should not touch the bottom of the container.
- Color the water but do not pour it into the container.

Activities

1. Have each student make a drawing to explain how he or she thinks the air in the balloon "escaped." Let students share these ideas. Give each student a tissue. Have them hold the tissues over their noses and mouths and then breathe through them. Ask students how they think the air got through the tissue. (The tissue is filled with tiny holes through which the air can pass.)

2. Show the students the empty container with the tubes in it. Have all the students observe what happens when the colored water is poured into the container. (The liquid travels up the tubes. The thinner the tube, the higher the water rises.)

Closure

- Show the transparency How Plants Get Their Food (page 29) and use it to explain what happened to the air in the balloon and the water in the tubes.
- Explain that green plants make their food by a process called photosynthesis. This process takes place mostly in the leaves. Chlorophyll in the leaves interacts with the water and dissolved minerals from the soil, carbon dioxide from the air, and light from the sun to produce food.

Taking in Food *(cont.)*

How Plants Get Their Food

By the Process of Osmosis

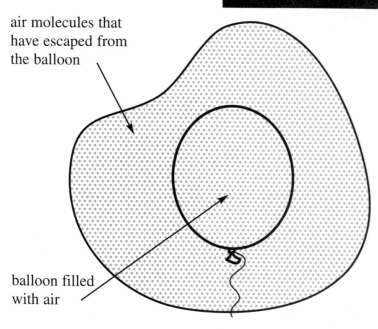

air molecules that have escaped from the balloon

balloon filled with air

magnified view of the balloon skin showing the tiny holes between the molecules that make up the skin (Molecules of air slowly escape through these holes.)

The plant cells that make up the roots have holes between them, just like the skin of the balloon. Water passes between these cells, carrying dissolved minerals into the plant.

Through Capillary Action

colored water level in tube

colored water level in container

The water rises higher as the tubes get thinner. This is how water moves through the tubes inside plant stems and leaves. Water molecules cling to the walls of the tubes and "climb" up them. As the molecules stretch upward, the top of the water dips.

Let's Make a Flower

Teacher Information

Students will each create their own model of a flower. They will make a cross section of the flower and glue or tape it to a piece of construction paper. This should be included in their plant journal.

Overview: *Students will make a model of a flower.*

Materials for the Flower Model

- green construction paper (stem and leaves)
- construction paper (petals)
- cotton swabs (stamens)
- variety of ground spices such as mustard, nutmeg, cinnamon (pollen)
- poppy seeds (seeds)
- 3" x 5" (8 cm x 13 cm) colored, unlined file card
- construction paper (on which to glue flower parts)

Other Materials

- Flower Dissection Instructions (page 24)
- Parts-of-a-Flower Data Sheet (page 25)
- transparency of page 26
- scissors
- clear tape
- white glue

Activity

1. Review the parts of a flower, using the information on pages 24–26. Discuss what students found as they dissected their flowers. Tell the students that they are going to make a model of a cutaway view of a flower.

2. Divide the students into small groups and provide them with the flower materials. Explain how the materials are to be used to represent the parts of the flower. The cotton swabs (stamens) should be dipped into white glue, and then one of the ground spices is sprinkled over the glue. These are left to dry before being added to the flower. The stigma should be drawn as an outline on the file card and be 5 inches (13 cm) long.

3. Tell students that they should follow the picture of the cutaway view of the flowers on pages 24 and 26. The flowers should be at least nine inches (23 cm) in length so details can be shown. They should glue all parts of the flower onto a sheet of construction paper.

4. Each student should make his or her own flower model. Encourage the students to be creative rather than making their flowers look exactly like the picture or another student's flower.

5. Have students put labels beside their flower with arrows to show where each part is located.

Closure

- Have students make models of their bean plants using construction paper. They should create their own leaves, stems, and roots and paste these to a sheet of paper.
- Post the flower and plant models on the bulletin board so the students can enjoy them.

Making a Plant Journal

Overview: *Students will create a cover for their plant journal.*

Materials

- light-colored file folder for each student
- colored pens or crayons
- all data sheets completed by the students from this study
- flower and plant models

Lesson Preparation

- Draw a large circle on the outside of each file folder.

Activity

1. Discuss what the students have learned about the life cycles of plants. Remind them of their observations of plant growth as they grew beans and birdseed. Also, remind them of what they learned about how seeds are formed as they dissected the flowers. Compare the life cycle of plants to those of insects so students see that there are similarities.

2. Tell them that they are going to make a cover for a plant journal in which they can place all the data sheets they have made during their study of plants. Distribute a file folder to each student. Tell them to draw the life stages of a plant around the circle, beginning with a cutaway view of a seed. Explain that their drawings of each stage should be large enough to show details.

(*Note:* If the students are not capable of doing this alone, divide the task into segments. Have them draw the seed, young plant, mature plant, and flower as you monitor their progress.)

Closure

- Let students share their pictures of the life cycles of plants. Have them add the title "My Plant Journal" to the covers of their journals.

- Have students make drawings of some of the plants which were cloned (e.g., carrot) on the back of their covers.

- Enclose all the data sheets and models in the plant journals.

The Importance of Bees

Teacher Information

Fossil bees have been found trapped in nectar and may have lived up to 80 million years ago. Bees most likely developed from wasp-like ancestors that ate other insects. Gradually, they switched to flower nectar for their food. Scientists believe that bees have helped create a wide variety of flowering plants in the world, by spreading pollen among the plants.

Bees live in nearly every part of the world except the North and South Poles. They make honey, which people eat, and beeswax, which is used in candles, adhesives, lipstick, chewing gum, and other useful things. Plants such as fruits and vegetables depend upon bees to pollinate them so they can reproduce seeds. As you can see, the bee is a very important and useful insect. There are about 20,000 different kinds of bees. Only the honeybee makes honey and wax.

There are solitary bees and social bees. Most bees are solitary, such as the carpenter, leafcutting, mining, and mason bees. Solitary bees usually live alone while social bees live in colonies that have as few as ten or as many as 80,000 members. Honeybees seem to have the most highly developed societies. Stingless bees and bumblebees are less social than honeybees. Stingless bees build nests in trees, on walls, in crude hives, or in the open. They may have from 50 to tens of thousands in their colonies. The bumblebee builds colonies of 50 to several hundred bees in the ground.

Overview: *Students learn about the history and anatomy of bees.*

Materials

- transparency of Anatomy of a Worker Honeybee (page 33)

Activity

1. Review the information about the importance of bees and plants which students learned in the lessons about flowers.

2. Share the information (above) about bees with the students. Emphasize that bees are extremely important since they pollinate plants. Without bees, many plants would not be able to produce fruit which we eat and which also contain the seeds for more plants.

3. Show the students the transparency of a bee and discuss the details of its body.

Closure

- Discuss bee "experiences" the students have had.

- Explain that in the next lesson, students will have the opportunity to see bees in action around the school grounds.

The Importance of Bees *(cont.)*

Anatomy of a Worker Honeybee

These detailed pictures show the body parts of a honeybee and explain their functions.

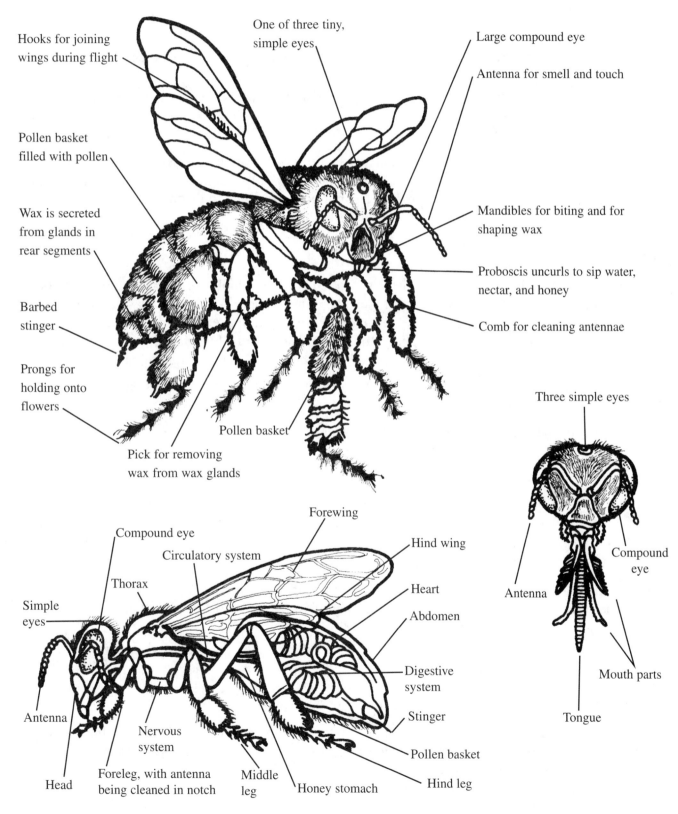

Hooks for joining wings during flight

One of three tiny, simple eyes

Large compound eye

Antenna for smell and touch

Pollen basket filled with pollen

Wax is secreted from glands in rear segments

Mandibles for biting and for shaping wax

Proboscis uncurls to sip water, nectar, and honey

Comb for cleaning antennae

Barbed stinger

Prongs for holding onto flowers

Pollen basket

Pick for removing wax from wax glands

Three simple eyes

Forewing

Compound eye

Circulatory system

Hind wing

Thorax

Heart

Simple eyes

Abdomen

Antenna

Antenna

Digestive system

Compound eye

Nervous system

Stinger

Mouth parts

Head

Foreleg, with antenna being cleaned in notch

Middle leg

Honey stomach

Pollen basket

Hind leg

Tongue

Looking at Bees

Overview: *Students observe bees on the school grounds and neighborhood.*

Materials

- area near the school where bees gather
- *optional:* video, regular, or digital camera
- *alternative option:* Show a film or video of bees gathering nectar. (Do this especially if even one student in class has a bee allergy.)

Caution: Before taking this field trip, be sure that none of the students have an allergy to bees.

Lesson Preparation

- Scout the school area when the sun is shining for flowers that are being visited by bees. Practice observing the bees in order to help the students know how this is done. Slowly approach bees that are gathering nectar and look at their hind legs for pollen clinging to them. Watch to see their behavior patterns as they move from one flower to the next.

Activity

1. Tell the students they are going on a bee hunt to see what bees look like and how they gather their food (nectar) from flowers. Explain that they are going to come close to the bees but will not be harmed if they do not disturb them. Explain that the eye of a bee sees a blurred image but it can detect movement thus, the students should remain still and calm while watching the bees. Assure the students that the bees are more interested in gathering food than stinging them.

2. Discuss what students will look for during the field trip. Ask students to focus on the following points:

   - how the bee approaches and enters the flower and how the wings move
   - how pollen is collected in the pollen baskets on the hind legs as well as on the body
   - noise the bee's wings may make as they move so fast they are a blur
   - which flowers the bees seem to like best

3. If a camera is available, take it along on the field trip to record what is observed.

Closure

- Return to the classroom and have the students break into small groups to discuss what they saw on the field trip. Have each group tell something they observed. List these on the board as a summary of their observations.
- Have the students make drawings of the bees. If available, show the picture record of the field trip.

Extender

- Check in the telephone book or contact a local nursery to find a beekeeper and invite him or her to class to describe their work to the students. If possible, arrange a field trip to the area of the beehives tended by the beekeeper.
- Serve a variety of flavors of honey to the students.

The Story of the Honeybee

To the Teacher: This activity is a shadow puppet show that simulates life in a honeybee colony.
Note: Although queen and worker bees are female, roles need to be assigned according to your classroom needs. If there are not enough students for all the parts in the play, some may take more than one role as reader or puppeteer.

Readers Needed	Puppets Needed
(1) queen	queen (1)
(4) workers A, B, C, D	worker bees (4)
(3) scouts, A, B, C	scout bees (3)
(3) guards A, B, C	guard bees (3)
(1) stagehand for background transparencies (pages 38–41)	wasp (1)
	top view of bee (1)

Materials

transparencies of puppets and scenery (pages 37– 41); 14 feet (1.5 m) of 22-or 24-gauge wire; hot-glue gun; yellow, orange, brown, green, and blue felt pens; puppet theater; overhead projector; large white butcher paper *(Wire may be purchased at a hardware or craft store.)*

Lesson Preparation

* See page 36 for explanation and diagrams.

Procedure

* Select the script readers, puppeteers, and stagehand. Readers will read the script as the play unfolds. Puppeteers manipulate the puppets, holding them close to the screen to focus them and moving the puppets as suggested in the script. Directions are in italics to the left of the script.

* It will take practice for students to discover the right distance their puppets need to be from the screen so the image is in focus. They also need to learn how to stay low so shadows of their bodies are out of the light and only the puppets and background scenery cast shadows on the screen. Help students coordinate the action of their puppets and the scenery with the script.

Closure

* After the students have developed their skills in presenting the shadow puppet play, let them present it to the class.

* Rotate other students into the roles so they have the opportunity to participate.

Extender

* Present the play to other classes in the school. Add background music, such as *The Flight of the Bumble Bee* or other appropriate music suggested by the story.

* Let students add to the script, using information from reference books. (See page 48 for references.)

The Story of the Honeybee *(cont.)*

Lesson Preparation: The shadow puppet stage may be created from a refrigerator box. Cut off the lids and one wide side of the box. Use the outer two sides as wings for the puppet theater. Cut a large rectangular hole near the top of the wide center panel and cover it with butcher paper. The paper becomes the screen for the puppet shadows. The audience sits on one side of the theater as the puppeteers work on the other (see drawing below). Transparencies of the scenery are placed on the stage of the overhead projector. Puppets are also made on transparencies which are then cut out and attached to a 12-inch (30 cm) length of wire.

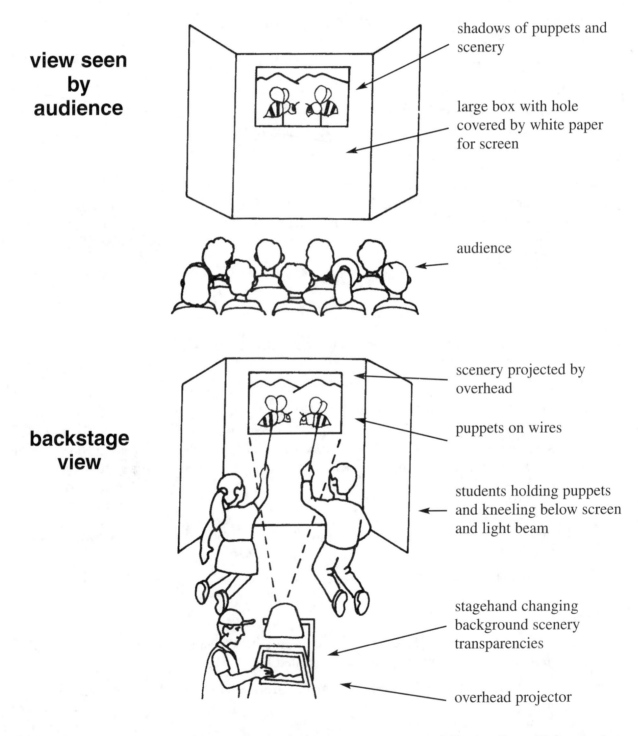

view seen by audience

shadows of puppets and scenery

large box with hole covered by white paper for screen

audience

backstage view

scenery projected by overhead

puppets on wires

students holding puppets and kneeling below screen and light beam

stagehand changing background scenery transparencies

overhead projector

Bee Puppets

To the Teacher: Make transparencies of the puppets and cut them out without the captions. These are used only to identify the puppets for the puppeteer. The number of puppets needed for each picture is shown in parentheses beside the name.

Use the hot-glue gun to attach the wire with tiny drops of hot glue to hold the puppets in a vertical position. The bees with wings that appear to be moving are used when they are flying during the play, such as the Scout A on page 44 of the script.

Queen (1)

Worker (4)

Drone (1)

Worker (1)
top view

Scout (3)

Wasp (1)

Guard (3)

The Story of the Honeybee *(cont.)*

Play Scenery

To the Teacher: Make transparencies of the scenery and cut them out to make individual pictures. Do not include captions which are to be used only in coordinating the pictures with the script. Prior to making transparencies, enlargement of these pictures may be needed to match the size of the puppets. This will prevent the necessity of changing the location of the projector during the performance.

Honeycomb with Queen and Worker Bees

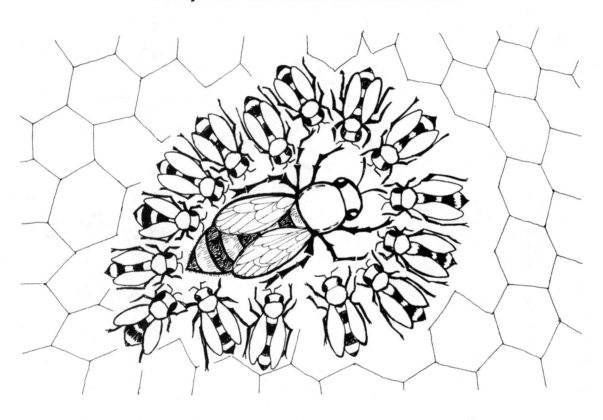

Development of a Bee

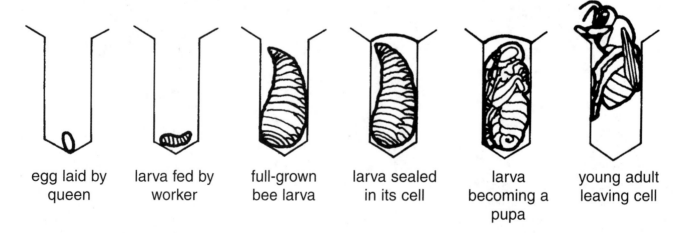

| egg laid by queen | larva fed by worker | full-grown bee larva | larva sealed in its cell | larva becoming a pupa | young adult leaving cell |

The Story of the Honeybee (cont.)

Play Scenery (cont.)

Use felt pens to color the meadow scene appropriately (color flowers blue in meadow). Make a duplicate of the flower field image. Use felt pens to color one copy with yellow petals and orange centers; the other should be blue petals with dark blue centers.

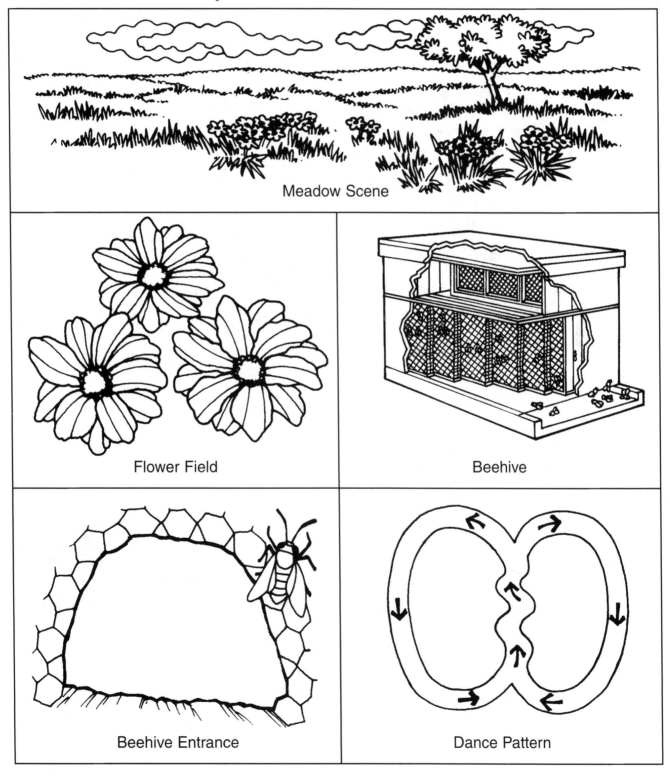

Meadow Scene

Flower Field

Beehive

Beehive Entrance

Dance Pattern

Play Scenery (cont.)

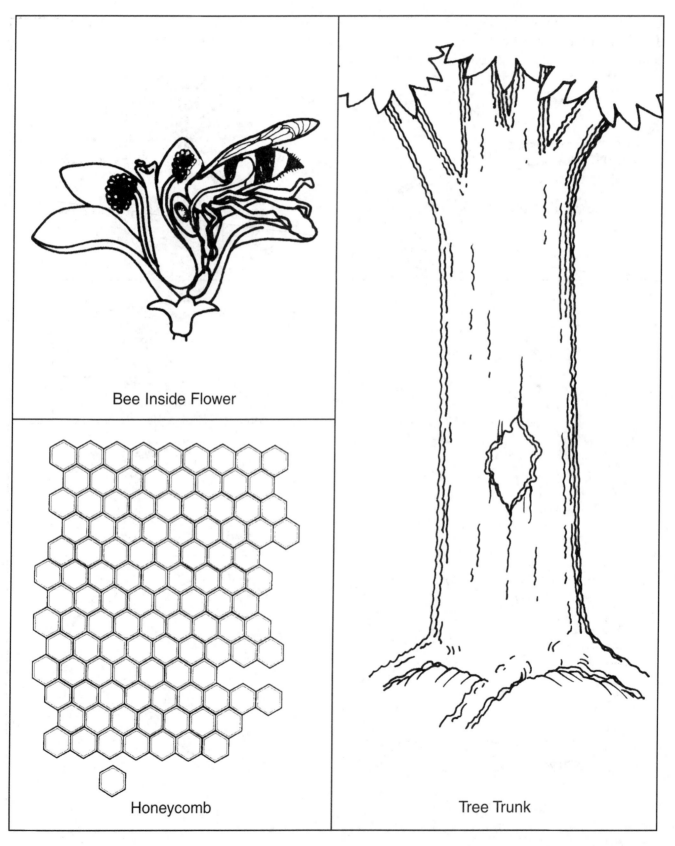

Bee Inside Flower

Honeycomb

Tree Trunk

Play Scenery *(cont.)*

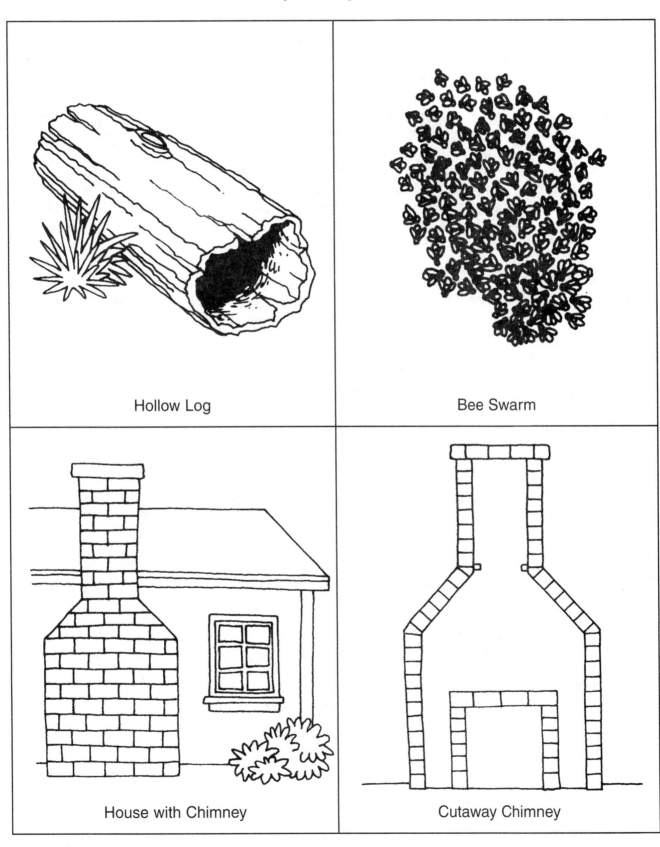

Hollow Log

Bee Swarm

House with Chimney

Cutaway Chimney

——————————————— **Puppet Play Script** ———————————————

Queen Bee:
(cutaway beehive)

Hello and welcome to my home, which is located inside this special box built by human beekeepers. It is called a *hive* and is a perfect place for my entire colony.

(honeycomb with queen and workers)

I'm the queen bee. That's me on the honeycomb. I'm the largest and the most important bee in the hive. I laid all the eggs, and so I am mother to everyone living in this colony. I am really busy laying eggs, now that it's spring. Sometimes I lay as many as 2,000 in one day! I hope you are impressed. There are almost 60,000 of my offspring living in this hive by now. Of course, as a queen bee all I do is eat lots of great honey and lay tens of thousands of eggs. If I'm healthy and well cared for, I could live for five years.

(queen bee puppet, honeycomb)

We are honeybees and live together in a colony, so we are called *social bees.* I want you to meet the bees which really do all the work around this colony. Naturally, they are called *worker bees.*

Worker A:
(queen bee and workers on honeycomb)

Hi! I'm Sally, one of the worker bees in this colony. My job is to build and repair the honeycomb. You can see me building it with the help of some of the other worker bees. We make each tubelike cell with six sides, which is a *hexagon,* so they fit snugly together.

(worker bee puppet)

I make the wax by eating lots of honey, and then glands in my body turn the sugar in the honey to wax. It oozes out of pores in my abdomen in tiny flakes. I pick off the flakes with my legs and pass them out to my mouth where I can chew them in my strong jaws. Finally, I pack the wax together with my mouth to form the cells.

(Place strip of pictures on projector stage showing development of a bee. Cover all but the pictures showing the queen laying eggs. Gradually uncover the next picture as the script calls for it.)

Queen Bee:
(egg and queen bee puppet in honeycomb cell)

Some of the workers are in charge of the nursery where they take care of the eggs I lay. *(Show queen laying egg in cell.)* First, I lay an egg in each cell of the wax cell honeycomb.

(larva in cell and worker bee puppet)

After three days, a tiny white wormlike larva will hatch from each egg, and the nurse worker bees will feed them.

Puppet Play Script *(cont.)*

Worker B:
(worker puppet)

I'm Martha, one of the nurse bees. You can see me feeding the larva a special diet of brood food which I make with glands in my head. This brood food is creamy and very rich in vitamins and proteins. After three days, I feed the larva a kind of bee bread which is a mixture of honey and pollen.

(pupa in cell)

The larva grows so big it fills the cell.

I seal the cell closed with some wax.

(pupa in cell)

The larva changes into a pupa and goes through a *metamorphosis,* which means a change. Gradually, the larva becomes an adult bee.

(adult leaving cell)

The adult bee will chew its way out of the cell and join the work force. We need all the help we can get!

Scout A:
(flying bee puppet, meadow scene)

I'm a scout worker bee which has been sent to find flowers where we can get nectar and pollen for food. I fly in bigger and bigger circles from the hive until I find the flowers. My special eyes will help me see them. I have five eyes! Three tiny ones form a triangle on the top of my head, and two huge bulging eyes are located on each side of my head. Can you see them? These are called compound eyes since they are made up of thousands of lenses packed together. The views from the thousands of lenses in my eyes combine to make one image which is somewhat blurred. My eyes are really great at seeing motion, however.

(yellow flowers and bee puppet)

Look at these flowers I am heading toward. You see them as yellow.

(blue flowers)

I see them like this because I see the ultraviolet light colors in them that you can't see. I can also locate the sun, even if it is a cloudy day. I need to know the sun's location so I can return to the hive and let my sister worker bees know just where to come to collect the food.

I'll fly back to the hive now and do my waggle dance to show them how to find the flowers.

— **Puppet Play Script** *(cont.)* —

Guard A:

(hive entrance, three guard puppets)

(flying bee, hive entrance)

(guards sniffing bee)

My name is Maria. I am a guard worker bee, and I make sure nothing comes into the hive except members of my family. These are some of my sisters who help me.

Look out, here comes a bee now! Come on, girls, we need to use our antennae to see if she smells like us. If she doesn't, we'll have to fight her so she can't invade our hive.

You smell OK. Let her pass. Imagine how impossible it would be to know each member of our family by sight since we all look alike. That's why our mother, Queen Cleopatra, passes around a *pheromone,* or scent, to each of us so we all smell alike and we know who belongs in this colony.

Scout A:

(honeycomb with dance pattern on top, top view of bee puppet)

Worker C:

(entrance of hive, bee puppets flying)

(blue flower field, three flying bee puppets)

Worker D:

(bee inside flower)

(flying bees)

OK, Girls, watch my dance. I'm going to show you just where I discovered the flowers. Now, I'll repeat the dance for you. Notice how I waggle toward the left; that means my sister bees will fly to the left of the sun to find the flowers.

I think we know just where to fly now. Follow me, girls. We are really working hard to fly with these heavy bodies of ours. Our wings flap about 250 times per second, and our top speed is 15 mph! We can fly forward, backward, and hover just like a helicopter.

There are the flowers! We will use our ultraviolet vision to see just where to land on the flowers to collect nectar.

Watch how I get down inside this flower and use my long tube-like tongue as a straw to drink the nectar into my honey stomach. My body is furry, so I also get covered with the sticky pollen which is on the tips of the stamen inside these flowers. I'll scrape the pollen off and put it into the pollen baskets on my back legs. Can you see the pollen I have already collected? Some of this pollen will fall off when I go to the next flower, but that is good since it helps the flower make seeds which become new plants. You call this process *pollinating* the plants. Bees are about the best pollinators on Earth! Many of the fruits and vegetables you eat depend upon us to continue growing.

=========== **Puppet Play Script** *(cont.)* ===========

Worker D: *(cont.)* It's time for us to fly back to the hive with our loads of nectar and pollen to pack it into the honeycomb cells.

Guard B:
(entrance with three guard bees) Be alert, girls—incoming bees! We need to give them the sniff test. You smell just right, so you can go inside.

Worker D:
(bees on top of honeycomb) I'll pump up the nectar from my stomach through my tongue into this cell. Now, I'll add some chemical enzymes to it. Other worker bees will fan the nectar to evaporate the water so it will turn into honey. We eat this honey for energy. The beekeeper collects the honey so you can eat it too. There is plenty of honey for all of us.

(bee puppet on honeycomb) I'm shaking the pollen out of the baskets on my hind legs into this cell. This pollen will give us the fat, proteins, vitamins, and minerals we need in our diet. *(Shouting)* Oh no! I smell the banana scent the guard bees give off when there is danger. Bee alert! Everyone to the entrance! We have to help guard the hive!

Guard C:
(wasp and three guard bees at entrance) You're not coming into my hive!

There go two of our brave sisters stinging and killing the wasp. The hooks on the ends of the stingers will make them stay inside the wasp's body. It's sad that our sister bees will die when the stingers are pulled out of their bodies, but they have saved all the rest of us.

Queen Bee:
(honeycomb with queen and workers) Whew! That attack was a close call, but the guards were courageous and saved us.

I've been in this hive for a long time, and it's time for me to leave and start a new home. I'll take a few thousand workers with me to help. There will soon be a new queen bee coming out of one of these cells. The nurse bees have been feeding it a special rich royal jelly so it will become larger and can take over my duties.

(queen bee and worker puppets, hive entrance) Fly with me, we'll find a tree so we can gather and set up a temporary headquarters while the scout bees look for a new location for our colony.

Puppet Play Script *(cont.)*

Worker B:
(larvae in cells and worker bee puppet)

You may have noticed that all the bees you have heard from so far were females.

There are very few males in our colony, and their only job is to mate with a queen so she can produce eggs. The larvae in these cells will become male bees, called *drones*. When they become adults, they will leave the hive to look for a queen from another nest so they can mate with her. After that, their job is done and they will die.

(two guard puppets, dragging one drone out of the entrance)

If there are any leftover drones in our hive when winter comes, the workers will drag them out of the hive. This may sound very cruel, but our food supplies run low in the winter when there are few or no flowers around. The drones can't even feed themselves on flower nectar since their tongues are too short, so we would have to feed them from our stored food during the winter. It is more important to feed it to the worker bees because we keep the rest of the colony members alive.

Scout A:
(bee-swarm in tree, three scout bee puppets)

The scouts have been sent to look for a new home for us. The queen will stay behind with the workers that will protect her during our search. Each of us will look for a different homesite and then return to the swarm and do a dance to show directions to our new locations.

(hollow tree, scout bee inside)

Look, I think that would be a good spot! *(The scout should cover her mouth with cupped hands to make it sound as if she is speaking into a hollow area.)* This looks like a great spot in here. I'll return to the swarm to tell the others about it. *(Scout bee flies back to swarm.)*

(Show tree with swarm and place the dance pattern under the picture in the region of the tree trunk. Use the top view of bee puppet to perform the dance.)

Scout A:

This is how you get to the tree I found. Let's go check it out.

Scout B:
(hollow tree, three bee puppets)

I don't think this will be a safe place for us. We need one which has a smaller entrance so it is easier to protect. Follow me to the one I found in a hollow log.

Scout C:
(hollow log)

(Talk into cupped hands.) This is too close to the ground. It could be invaded by skunks or other insects. Come with me to check out the great place I found.

Scout B:
(house with chimney)

This is a great place! The entrance is small so it's easy to protect, and the wind and rain can't get inside. We can build the nest higher up the chimney so warm air won't escape. It also faces south, so the sun will keep us warm inside here.

Scout A:
(cutaway chimney, bee puppet inside)

(Talk into cupped hands.) The size is just right—large enough to hold the honeycomb we need but not too big for us to keep it warm. I think we should fly back to the swarm and bring the others here.

Scout C:
(swarm of bees laid on projector stage, bee puppets flying)

We have found a perfect place for our new home. Follow me—I'll lead the way.

(Scout flies back to swarm to encourage them to keep together.) Stay together everyone! I'll show you the right way to go.

Queen Bee:
(chimney, bees entering)

(Talk into cupped hands.) Wow! You did a great job. This will make a perfect home for our new colony. Everyone set to work making the honeycomb! I need to get busy laying more eggs to expand my family again.

Teacher and Student Resources

Related Books

Barrett, Katharine and Carolyn Willard. *Schoolyard Ecology*. 1999. Order through GEMS. (See suppliers listed below.) This teacher's guide provides a wealth of activities for students in grades 3–6 to do in their own school area to discover how the plants and animals co-exist there.

Cole, Joanna. *The Magic School Bus® Inside a Beehive*, Scholastic, Inc., 1996. Ms. Frizzle takes her students on a field trip adventure to a beehive where they students and teacher turn into bees. They learn about the life of bees during this great trip.

Barber, Jacqueline and Kimi Hosoume. *Terrarium Habitats*, 2000. Order through GEMS. (See suppliers listed below.) The activities in this guide bring this hidden world up close, deepening student understanding of and connection to all living things. The activities are designed for students in grades K–6.

Young, Ruth M. *Science Literature Unit: The Magic School Bus® Inside a Beehive*. Teacher Created Resources, 1997. This teacher's guide is filled with activities that bring to life the experience Ms. Frizzle's students have on their unusual field trip to a beehive. (See Joanna Cole book above.)

Suppliers of Science Materials

Delta Education (800) 282-9560. Request a catalog of materials or order online at their web site.
http://www.delta-education.com/corp/info/ordernow.html
Supplies a wide variety of materials to support hands-on science in all areas from elementary to middle school. These include books and materials about plants such as live Venus's-flytrap plants.

Great Explorations in Math and Science (GEMS)
http://www.lhs.berkeley.edu/GEMS/gemsguides.html
Directly from the Lawrence Hall of Science at UC Berkeley comes great teacher guides in a wide range of science topics. Check out their web site to see all that is available.

National Science Resource Center **http://www.si.edu/nsrc/**
Resources for Teaching Elementary Science. National Science Resource Center, National Academy Press, Washington, D.C., 1996. This outstanding resource guide to hands-on inquiry-centered elementary science curriculum materials and resources. Each reference in this guide has been carefully evaluated and is fully described, including addresses.
Read this book online or order it from **http://www.nap.edu/catalog/4966.html**

National Science Teachers Association (NSTA) (800) 277-5300
http://www.nsta.org/ or the online catalog of materials at **http://store.nsta.org/**
Provides books, posters, and software related to astronomy and other sciences.
A month professional journal, the bimonthly NSTA Reports, discounts at the regional and national conventions and annual catalog of materials.